LET THE ADVENTURES BEGIN!

Did you know that Ohio has 8 parks that are run by Rangers who work for the National Park Service (NPS)? Ohio has a lot of parks but most of them are run by the state of Ohio. Only 8 parks are run by Rangers who work for the NPS. These parks tell the story of people, places and things in Ohio that make the United States so special and unique.

NPS Rangers take care of parks that are owned by the citizens of the United States of America. This is the only country in the world where the people, not the government, own the public lands.

This is why it is important for you to know about these wonderful places...because they are your responsibility to care for and protect.

Rangers are at all of these parks and can tell you more and answer any questions you may have.

OHIO
National Parks, Monuments, and Historic Sites

THE ARROWHEAD was authorized as the official National Park Service emblem on July 20, 1951.

A NATIONAL PARK has at least one of the following: an outstanding feature, historical value, or natural phenomenon.

A NATIONAL MONUMENT generally contains objects of historic, prehistoric, or scientific interest.

OHIO STATE PARKS
Table of Contents

1. Charles Young Buffalo Soldiers National Monument 4
2. Cuyahoga Valley National Park 8
3. Dayton Aviation Heritage National Historical Park 12
4. First Ladies National Historic Site 16
5. Hopewell Culture National Historical Park 20
6. James A. Garfield National Historic Site 24
7. Perry's Victory and International Peace Memorial 28
8. William Howard Taft National Historic Site 32

Ohio State Interesting Facts 36

> **The mission of the National Park Service** is to preserve unimpaired the natural and cultural resources and values of the National Park System for the enjoyment, education, and inspiration of this and future generations.
> —nps.gov

CHARLES YOUNG BUFFALO SOLDIERS NATIONAL MONUMENT

- Dedicated on April 2, 2013
- Charles and Ada bought their home in 1907 and named it "Youngsholm"
- Located next to the campus of Wilberforce University

1120 US-42
Xenia, OH

CHARLES YOUNG BUFFALO SOLDIERS NATIONAL MONUMENT
Record Your Visit

Cancellation & Regional Stamp(s), photos, memories, etc.

CHARLES YOUNG BUFFALO SOLDIERS NATIONAL MONUMENT

Charles Young was **BORN A SLAVE** on March 12, 1864. His family crossed into Ohio shortly after his birth so that he could grow up in a free state.

Young could speak many languages and **PLAYED** the **PIANO, VIOLIN** and **GUITAR**.

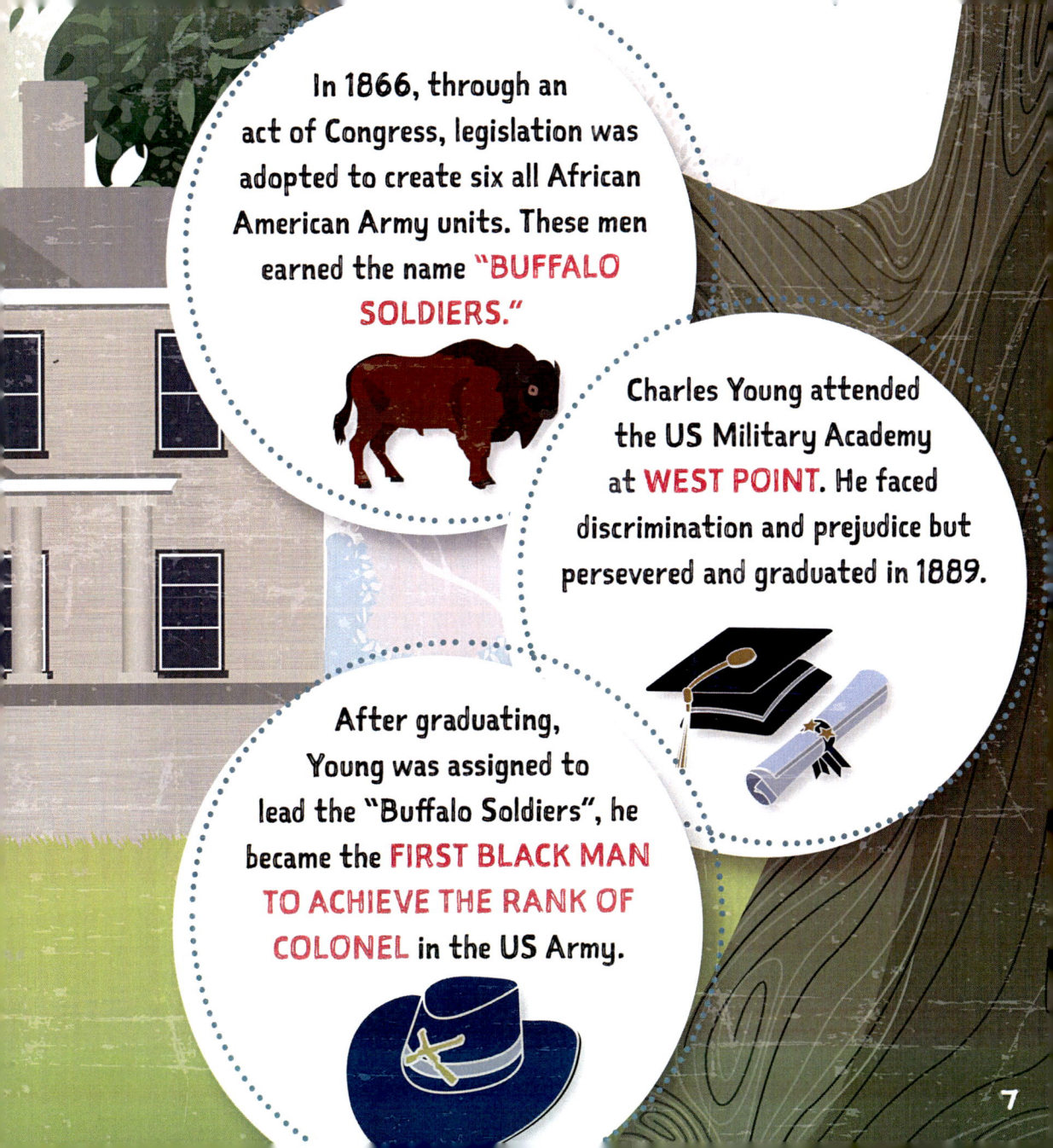

In 1866, through an act of Congress, legislation was adopted to create six all African American Army units. These men earned the name "BUFFALO SOLDIERS."

Charles Young attended the US Military Academy at WEST POINT. He faced discrimination and prejudice but persevered and graduated in 1889.

After graduating, Young was assigned to lead the "Buffalo Soldiers", he became the FIRST BLACK MAN TO ACHIEVE THE RANK OF COLONEL in the US Army.

CUYAHOGA VALLEY NATIONAL PARK

Boston Mills Visitor Center
6947 Riverview Road,
Peninsula, OH 44264

- Established in 2000

- 32,572 acre park & 51 square miles

- There are nearly 100 waterfalls in the Cuyahoga Valley

CUYAHOGA VALLEY NATIONAL PARK
Record Your Visit

Cancellation & Regional Stamp(s), photos, memories, etc.

If you look carefully, you might see a **YELLOW WARBLER**, especially in the spring and summer.

MINKS are excellent swimmers, you might be able to spot one on or near a body of water.

CUYAHOGA VALLEY NATIONAL PARK

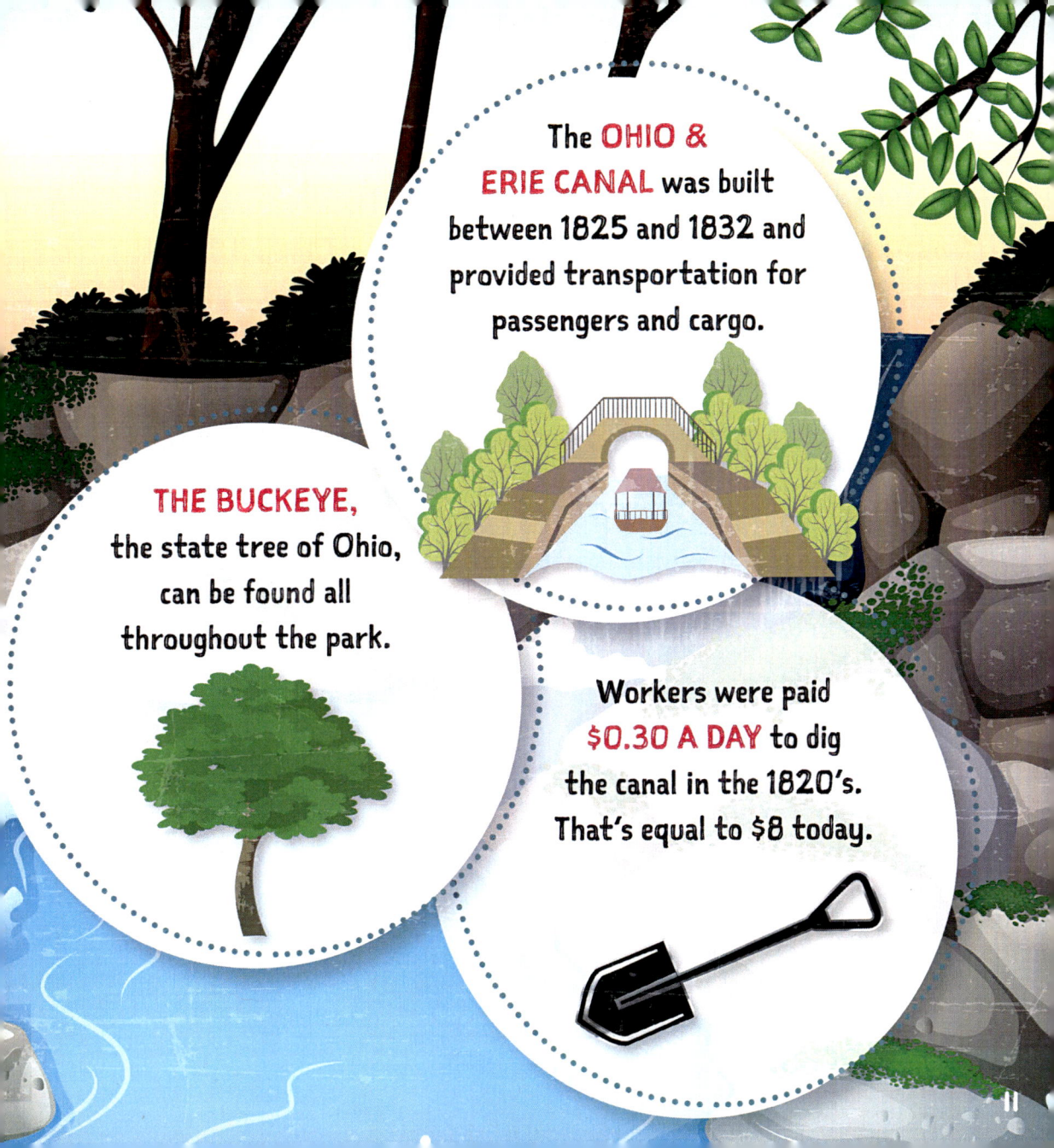

The **OHIO & ERIE CANAL** was built between 1825 and 1832 and provided transportation for passengers and cargo.

THE BUCKEYE, the state tree of Ohio, can be found all throughout the park.

Workers were paid **$0.30 A DAY** to dig the canal in the 1820's. That's equal to $8 today.

DAYTON AVIATION HERITAGE NATIONAL HISTORICAL PARK

- In 1903, the Wright brothers were the first to fly a powered airplane

- Authorized by Congress in October 1992

- Paul Dunbar, a famous Black writer from Dayton, and Orville Wright were classmates and business partners

3 16 S. Williams St.
Dayton, OH 45402

DAYTON AVIATION HERITAGE NATIONAL HISTORICAL PARK
Record Your Visit

This is the only place you can get a cancellation stamp from Mars!

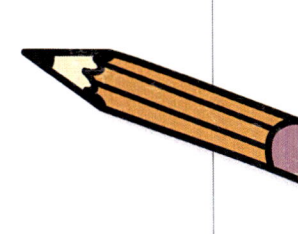

Cancellation & Regional Stamp(s), photos, memories, etc.

13

DAYTON AVIATION HERITAGE NATIONAL HISTORICAL PARK

At **HUFFMAN PRAIRIE FLYING FIELD**, the Wright brothers set world flying records and started the first pilot school.

A **BICYCLE** repair shop was one of the Wright brothers' first businesses.

PAUL DUNBAR was president of his school's literary society and the only black student in his graduating class of 1891 at Central High School in Dayton.

The Wrights and Dunbar worked together on the **TATTLER NEWSPAPER** in 1890 & 1891.

The Wright Brothers

Wilbur

Orville

Dunbar's most well known work is his poem, **SYMPATHY**, where he says: "I know why the caged bird sings."

FIRST LADIES NATIONAL HISTORIC SITE

205 Market Ave South, Canton Ohio 44702

- Authorized by Congress on October 11, 2000
- The site includes the Saxton House and the Education Center
- Seven First Ladies came from Ohio

FIRST LADIES NATIONAL HISTORIC SITE
Record Your Visit

Cancellation & Regional Stamp(s), photos, memories, etc.

FIRST LADIES NATIONAL HISTORIC SITE

FLORENCE AND WARREN HARDING owned an airedale terrier which was a hit with the public!

HELEN "NELLIE" HERRON TAFT inspired the First Ladies Gown exhibit by donating hers to the Museum of American History.

LUCY WEBB HAYES started the first White House Easter Egg roll. Have you ever rolled your eggs on Easter?

CAROLINE SCOTT HARRISON initiated extensive renovation of the White House, including the installation of electric lighting.

The First Lady **PERFORMS DUTIES AND SERVICES** recognized throughout the world.

HOPEWELL CULTURE NATIONAL HISTORICAL PARK

- Renamed by Congress on May 27, 1992 to include preservation of 5 separate earthwork locations

- Geometric earthworks and mounds of various sizes were built over 2,000 years ago

- An active archaeological site

16062 OH-104, Chillicothe, OH 45601

HOPEWELL CULTURE NATIONAL HISTORIC PARK
Record Your Visit

Cancellation & Regional Stamp(s), photos, memories, etc.

HOPEWELL CULTURE NATIONAL HISTORIC PARK

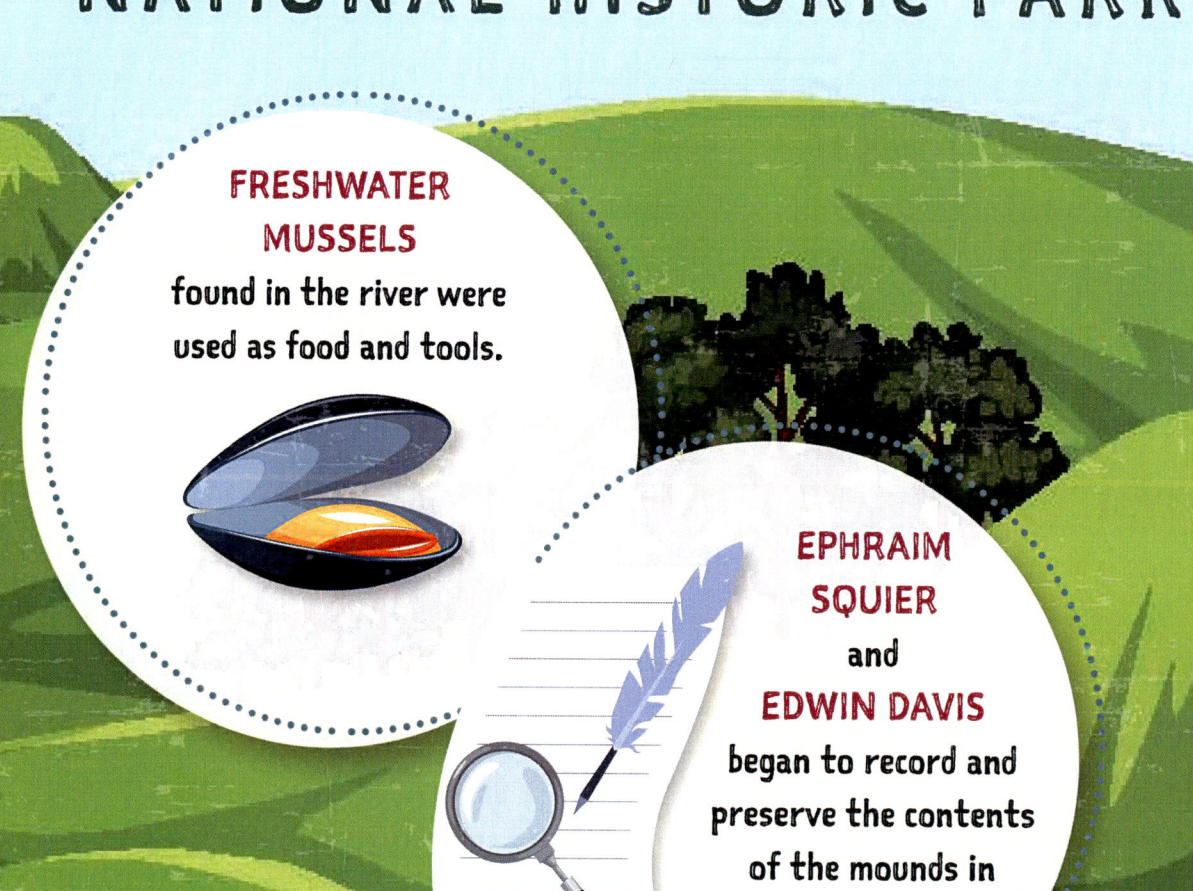

FRESHWATER MUSSELS found in the river were used as food and tools.

EPHRAIM SQUIER and **EDWIN DAVIS** began to record and preserve the contents of the mounds in the 1840's.

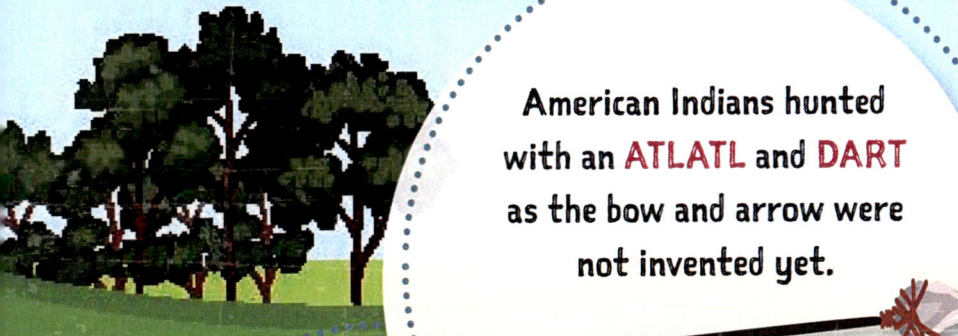

American Indians hunted with an **ATLATL** and **DART** as the bow and arrow were not invented yet.

An **ARTIFACT** is an ornament, tool, or other object that is made by a human being.

ARCHAEOLOGISTS study the human past to learn how and why people lived by analyzing the things they left behind.

JAMES A. GARFIELD NATIONAL HISTORIC SITE

8095 Mentor Ave.
Mentor, Ohio 44060

- James Garfield was the 20th president of the United States

- He was born in a log cabin in 1831

- His first job was as a mule driver

- Lucretia Garfield added a library to their home to honor his memory

JAMES A. GARFIELD NATIONAL HISTORIC SITE
Record Your Visit

Cancellation & Regional Stamp(s), photos, memories, etc.

JAMES A. GARFIELD NATIONAL HISTORIC SITE

Thousands of people stopped by to hear Garfield campaign from his **FRONT PORCH**.

Lucretia Garfield added a **WINDMILL** and many other buildings after her husband's death as she tried to create a more elegant Victorian estate.

While in **CONGRESS**, Garfield supported African-American suffrage and Public Education.

On July 2, 1881 president Garfield was **SHOT**, his wounds became infected, and he died on September 19, 1881.

JAMES GARFIELD was a teacher, principal, Ohio Senator, Civil War Officer, US Congressman and President.

PERRY'S VICTORY AND INTERNATIONAL PEACE

1 Bayview
Put-in-Bay, OH 43456

- The monument is 352 feet tall, about 30 school buses stacked!

- The monument was completed in 1915

- "DONT GIVE UP THE SHIP" flag was made to honor Commander James Lawrence

DONT GIVE UP THE SHIP

PERRY'S VICTORY AND INTERNATIONAL PEACE
Record Your Visit

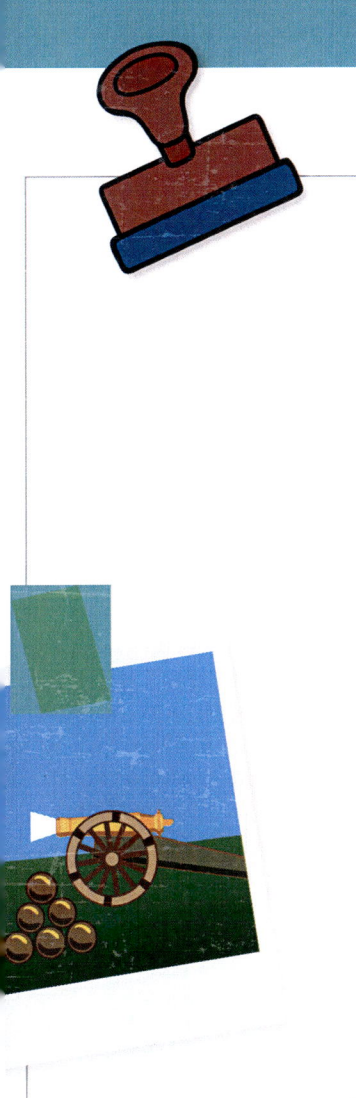

Cancellation & Regional Stamp(s), photos, memories, etc.

PERRY'S VICTORY AND INTERNATIONAL PEACE

PERRY'S VICTORY AND INTERNATIONAL PEACE Memorial celebrates the long-lasting peace among the United Kingdom, Canada, and the U.S.

The Memorial also celebrates those who fought in the **BATTLE OF LAKE ERIE** in the War of 1812.

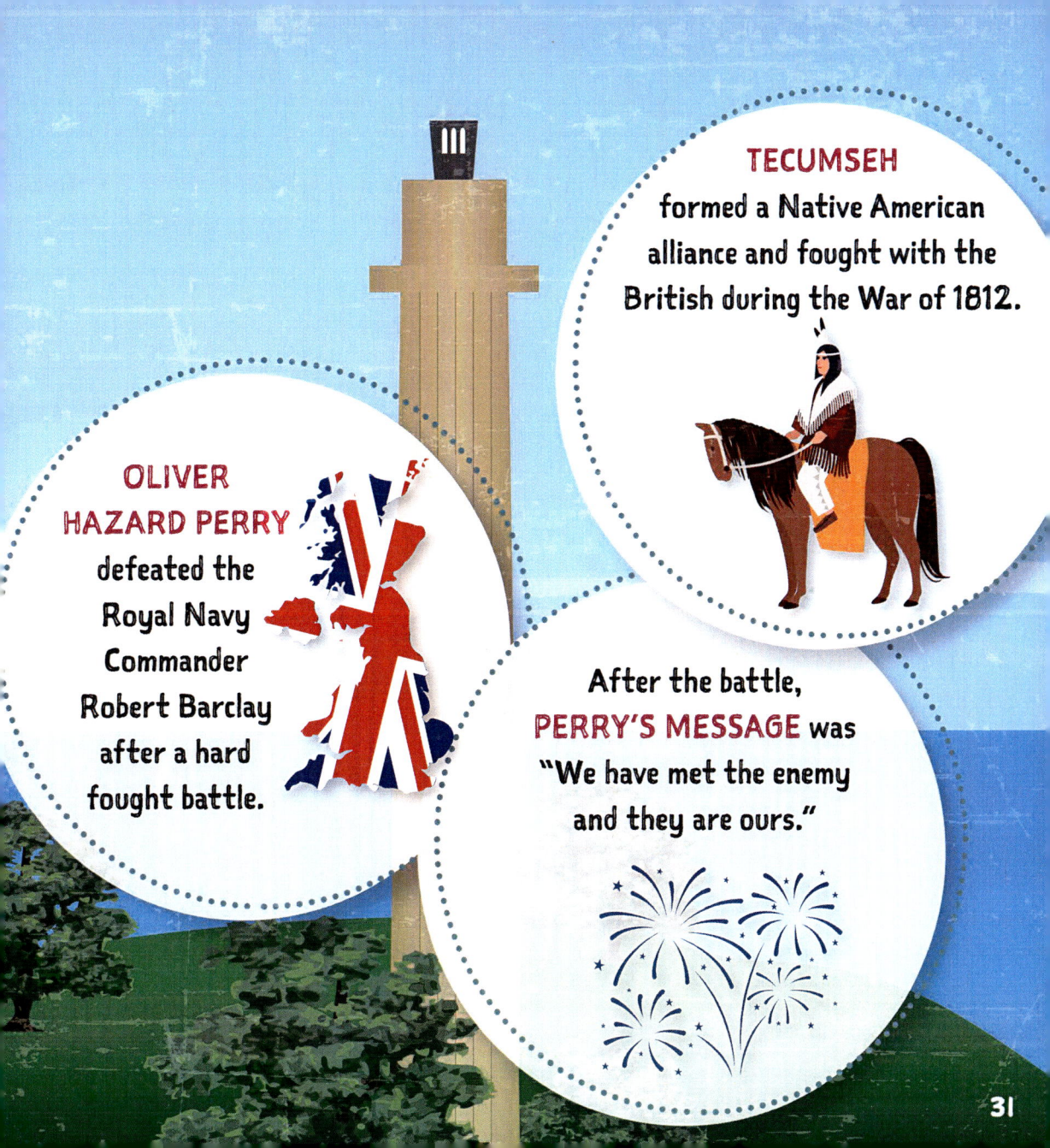

OLIVER HAZARD PERRY defeated the Royal Navy Commander Robert Barclay after a hard fought battle.

TECUMSEH formed a Native American alliance and fought with the British during the War of 1812.

After the battle, **PERRY'S MESSAGE** was "We have met the enemy and they are ours."

WILLIAM HOWARD TAFT NATIONAL HISTORIC SITE

- Established on December 2, 1969

- William Howard Taft was the 27th President of the U.S. from 1909-1913

- 10th Chief Justice of the Supreme Court

- Located at Taft's Birthplace

8 2038 Auburn Ave, Cincinnati, OH 45219

WILLIAM HOWARD TAFT NATIONAL HISTORIC SITE
Record Your Visit

Cancellation & Regional Stamp(s), photos, memories, etc.

WILLIAM HOWARD TAFT NATIONAL HISTORIC SITE

After graduating from Yale in 1878, Taft returned home to practice law but also **PURSUED POLITICS.**

Appointed **SECRETARY OF WAR** by President Teddy Roosevelt, Taft oversaw the construction of the Panama Canal.

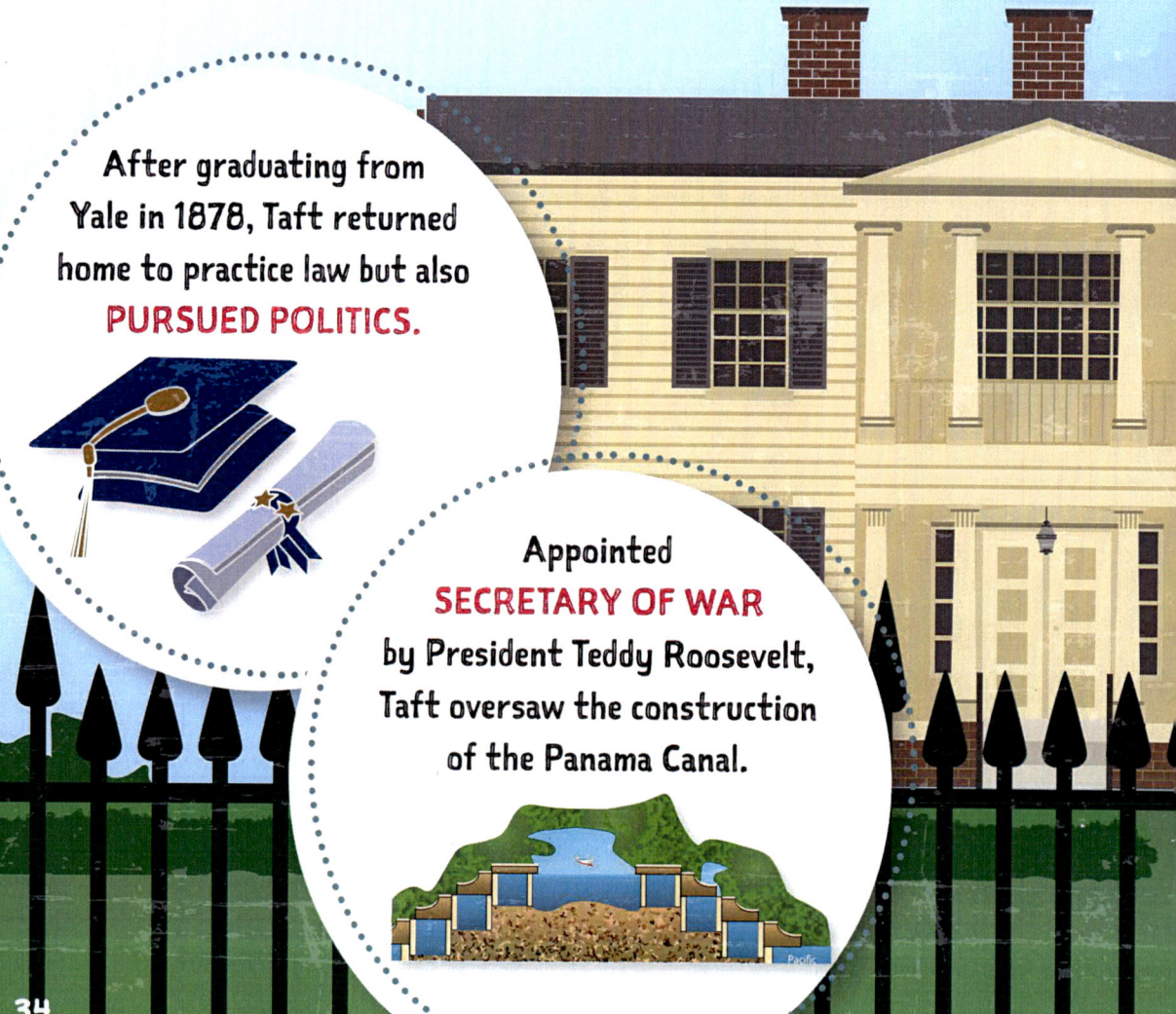

PRESIDENT THEODORE ROOSEVLT chose Taft as his successor for President.

Helen "Nellie" Taft orchestrated the planting of over **3,000 JAPANESE CHERRY TREES.**

Taft's greatest pleasure was being **SUPREME COURT JUSTICE** and he remained in office until shortly before his death.

OHIO STATE INTERESTING FACTS

The name Ohio originated from the Iroquois word **"OHI-YO"** which means "great river."

State Capital:

Columbus

We are grateful to the Ohio state park rangers for their invaluable feedback.